SLA GUIDELI

Access for Everyone

Supporting Special Needs Through the School Library

Dr Rona Tutt OBE

Series Editor: Geoff Dubber

Acknowledgements

The SLA Publications Team would like to thank our own Sally Duncan and Tricia Adams for reading and commenting on this text for us.

Published by

School Library Association
1 Pine Court, Kembrey Park
Swindon
SN2 8AD

Tel: 01793 530166   Fax: 01793 481182
E-mail: info@sla.org.uk
Web: www.sla.org.uk

Registered Charity No: 313660
Charity Registered in Scotland No: SC039453

ISBN: 978-1-903446-84-3

Printed by Holywell Press, Oxford

Contents

Introduction

The year 2014 saw the biggest shake up of the Special Educational Needs (SEN) system in schools for over 30 years. One of the results has been that SEN has gained a higher profile and this will remain the case until the new system is thoroughly embedded, which will take many years. There is a renewed emphasis and energy on finding ways of supporting children and young people who struggle with some, or all, aspects of school life and to do so as soon as possible. As becoming literate is central to success, school libraries have a key part to play in helping pupils to overcome some of the barriers to learning that they experience. They can also be places which provide a welcome respite from the strains and stresses of the classroom or playground, as well as giving pupils the desire to read and to learn.

The term 'SEN' was designed to cover the 20% or so of pupils who will have difficulty accessing the curriculum at some stage of their school career.

You may come across both the terms 'SEN' and 'SEND', the latter standing for SEN and disability. There is a very large overlap between the two terms, although there is a small percentage of children who have SEN but may not be seen as disabled, as well as a small number who are disabled, but do not have SEN.

The SEND Code of Practice which was published in July 2014, incorporated 'disability' into the definition of SEN in the previous Code (*Special Educational Needs Code of Practice*, 2001), so that it now reads:

> 'A child or young person has SEN if they have a learning difficulty or disability which calls for special educational provision to be made for them.' (p.15)

About 2.8% of pupils who have the most complex needs, have had a legal document called a 'statement', which sets out the provision that they need to support them. Under the new arrangements, this is called an Education, Health and Care Plan (EHC Plan).

A further explanation of what is included in the term 'SEN' is given in the first chapter of this book, which explains the various types of needs that fall within this overarching term. The second chapter explains how the SEN Framework is changing. These changes were signalled in October 2010, but are likely to take until at least April 2018 to be fully implemented. A change of government during this time could alter the timetable, but is unlikely to alter the content very much, as there is general agreement among the main political parties about the right way forward. Taken together, these two chapters provide the context for the later chapters, which cover some of the practical ways in which school libraries and those who work in them, can encourage pupils with SEN to make full use of the library and its facilities, as they move through the different key stages. Two case studies are included in these chapters. One is of a special school for primary aged pupils and the other is an academy for secondary students. The penultimate chapter goes wider than SEN, to include pupils whose behaviour may or may not be part of having a recognised special need. The final chapter lists some resources that have been mentioned and others that may be of interest.

In writing this book, I have been very aware that some schools and educational settings for younger children are unlikely to be fortunate enough to have a school librarian, whereas many secondary schools will have one. So I have tried to make the material relevant to everyone who is interested in their school library, regardless of the age of the pupils attending their school. Indeed, there is such a diversity of schools that some are neither primary nor secondary, but cover the whole age range. Although the title of some chapters would suggest they are aimed at librarians, this should not be taken as an indication that the chapters are only relevant to professional school librarians. Again, I have tried to make the information and ideas relevant to all those involved in running, organising, or developing their school libraries, whether as librarians, school leaders, teaching staff, support staff, parents, governors or volunteers.

The well-stocked, well-organised school library can be, indeed should be, a fantastic resource for pupils of all ages. For students who have SEN, it can be a particularly vital resource. Yet, the pupils who may benefit the most from being able to access a library at school, may also be the ones who, without the right sort of encouragement, may shun the attempts to lure them in. The reasons for this are many and varied. Some will see a place that is full of books as somewhere to be avoided at all costs, because they have found learning to read difficult and associate books with feelings of anxiety and failure. For others, the rather quiet, working atmosphere may not appeal to their hyperactive nature and they will view it as a dull place to be, without giving themselves the chance to explore what may well be a goldmine of enjoyment and information.

I hope that this publication will contribute to a greater understanding of SEN generally and provide some fresh ideas to maximise the use made of school libraries by all children and young people, but especially by those for whom learning is a challenge.

Chapter 1
What is meant by SEN?

The term *special educational needs* or *SEN* has been in use since the 1980s. It is a way of recognising the 20% or so of pupils who will need additional support for all or part of their school careers. It covers a very wide range, from those whose needs may be temporary, to those who have lifelong conditions which affect their ability to learn in school. Within the SEN continuum, the following types of need are well established:

General learning difficulties

General learning difficulties can also be described as global learning difficulties. These are the pupils who are likely to have difficulty in all areas of learning. They range from those who are simply below average in ability and struggle a little to keep up with their classmates, to those who have more significant needs and are said to have moderate learning difficulties (MLD), severe learning difficulties (SLD), or profound and multiple learning difficulties (PMLD).

Moderate learning difficulties (MLD)

There used to be a number of special schools for pupils who were assessed as having MLD, but, for some time now, the majority have been in mainstream schools, unless they have additional difficulties as well. These pupils are capable of enjoying learning, but need to go at a much slower pace than their peers and to have plenty of repetition in order to understand and remember what they have been taught. They find it harder to deal with abstract ideas. As they are often less mature than their peers, they may enjoy reading material aimed at a younger age group.

Severe learning difficulties (SLD)

Most of these pupils will be in schools for SLD and PMLD pupils, particularly as they get older and the gap between them and their peers continues to grow. Their ability to speak fluently and to take in what is said to them will be limited. Some will learn to read, although not always with understanding. This does not mean that they cannot enjoy having stories read to them and choosing books they want to look at. Indeed, listening to stories and being involved through role play, dressing up or handling objects to do with the stories, will help the experience to come alive for them.

Profound and multiple learning difficulties (PMLD)

These pupils are unlikely to be in mainstream schools because of the severity of their needs. Many are wheelchair users. They may have hearing and/or sight impairments as well and benefit from a sensory-based curriculum. Each one may have a different combination of needs, so classes are very small and there is a great deal of individual support. These schools, which usually cater for both SLD and PMLD pupils, are likely to have hydrotherapy pools, sensory rooms, soft play areas and many other adaptations to give space for wheelchair users and to provide a very specialised learning environment.

Specific Learning Difficulties (SpLD)

Unlike pupils who have general learning difficulties affecting all areas of learning, these pupils have particular difficulty with only some aspects of the curriculum and may well be average or above average in other subjects. The following types of SpLD are recognised:

Dyslexia

This is the most common form of SpLD and at one time the two terms were used almost interchangeably. There are many different reasons why pupils are dyslexic and the nature of their difficulties will vary, but they will all have problems with learning to read and to spell. This can be very frustrating if pupils are otherwise bright and cannot understand why they are falling behind their classmates. Depending on the severity of their condition, some may never become fluent readers, but books and reading can still be an important part of their lives. Those who are more mildly affected may be able to overcome their difficulties to the extent that they become avid readers. Because dyslexia can manifest itself in different ways, some pupils respond to having coloured overlays over the text, or prefer text on a less glossy white background.

Dyscalculia

This condition has received far less attention than dyslexia, but it can have a serious impact on many areas of learning. Most young children will pick up a sense of number quite early on, but a few seem to lack this basic understanding of what numbers mean and how they relate to the written symbols. These pupils will have difficulty understanding anything to do with numbers, as well as other mathematical concepts such as time, money, shape and space.

Dyspraxia

Also known as developmental co-ordination disorder (DCD), this condition results in pupils having difficulty controlling the muscles involved in movement. Formerly, they might have been described as being 'clumsy'. Both the large scale movements, such as running, jumping, throwing and catching, as well as the smaller movements involved in manipulating buttons, doing jigsaws, or using the right pencil grip, are likely to be affected.

Dysgraphia

This is the least known of the Specific Learning Difficulties. Unlike dyslexia, it does not affect reading, but only writing, both in terms of the physical act of handwriting and in terms of getting ideas down on paper. Sometimes, these pupils will move their upper body across the page as they write, as a way of trying to compensate for their difficulty in forming letters and words.

Speech, Language and Communication Needs (SLCN)

This is a broad term which covers pupils who are very delayed in their language development, as well as those who have a specific language impairment (SLI). Considerable concern has been expressed about children arriving in school unable to string words together in order to speak in sentences, or knowing how to hold a conversation. Many reasons have been put forward for this, including:

- the over-use of television from an early age
- the disappearance of conversation around the family dining table
- the lack of bedtime stories
- the rise in single parent families, or families where both parents go out to work.

In either of these latter scenarios, there may be less time for parents to spend talking with their children and helping to develop their language. Young children whose language development has been delayed by their home circumstances, often catch up once they are immersed in the rich language environment of the classroom and have access to books and to stories. However, this is not so true of children who have a specific language impairment.

Specific Language Impairment (SLI)

This term is used to describe pupils whose language development does not follow the normal pattern, rather than simply being delayed. They may have difficulty discriminating between the 44 sounds of the English language or being able to pronounce them all. They may find it difficult to follow the meaning of what is said to them, or struggle to understand non-literal language, such as *'Pull your socks up'* (when this is not what is literally meant), or responding to a rhetorical question, for example, *'Can you take the register to the office for me?'* when, instead of doing so, they may simply reply, *'Yes'!* (This difficulty with coping with non-literal language is also a feature of autism.) These pupils benefit enormously from the attention of a speech and language therapist or a specialist teacher in communication.

Autism

Autism is sometimes referred to as the autism spectrum, an autistic spectrum disorder (ASD), or autistic spectrum condition (ASC). The most marked areas of difficulty are in communicating, being sociable and being flexible in their thinking and behaviour. Children with autism may be hyposensitive (lacking in sensitivity) or hypersensitive (being over-sensitive). People who have autism can also find it hard to integrate information coming in from the different senses and so can feel overwhelmed by the amount of information they are receiving, without being able to piece it together. For instance, if a child with autism throws a tantrum in the supermarket, this might be because of the amount of noise, light and visual displays that overwhelm his or her senses.

The term autism includes **Asperger's syndrome**, where the same difficulties occur, but in a less obvious form. For instance, these pupils may be fluent talkers, but will want to talk about their particular interests rather than holding a conversation. They may want to be sociable, but lack social skills and so annoy other children by interfering with their activities or by wanting to dominate. They may be keen to devour books, particularly non-fiction, but on the topic or topics that interest them the most. This can make it difficult for those in charge of the library to have enough books on a particular topic, and is in contrast to children with the more severe form of autism (classic autism), who may want to read the same book over and over again. Younger children may have an obsession with *Thomas the Tank Engine* books, while older ones may go for *Dr Who*. Girls seem to be particularly attracted to Disney characters.

Behavioural, Emotional and Social Difficulties (BESD)

This description has been in use since the second version of the SEN Code of Practice was published in 2001. In the *SEND code of practice: 0-25 years*, it has been replaced by the term Social, Emotional and Mental Health Difficulties (SEMH). This used to describe a child or young person whose behaviour is such that it impacts on his or her ability to learn. It includes the very aggressive, disruptive pupil and the one who is unusually quiet and withdrawn, who may be unhappy as well.

The change is to encourage people to look beneath the behaviour at the reasons *why* children and young people are behaving in a certain way, rather than concentrating on the actual behaviour being exhibited. It also recognises that many children have mental health issues, a fact that has been slow to gain recognition. Pupils with SEN have been found to be particularly vulnerable to developing mental health problems.

Attention Deficit Hyperactivity Disorder (ADHD)

One of the most usual types of difficulty in this area is ADHD. There are three characteristics that are used to identify this condition:

- being unusually impulsive
- inattentive
- and hyperactive.

Many young children will display these characteristics from time to time, but pupils with ADHD are like it for most of the time, whether they are at home or at school. They are inclined to act before thinking rather than the other way round. They find it hard to sit still without fidgeting or to concentrate on an activity for any length of time. There is a debate about whether they should be given medication to help them to settle down and learn. In more severe cases, it may be necessary, but whether or not pupils receive medication, they need to be taught strategies to try to help them to overcome their difficulties.

Attention Deficit Disorder (ADD)

Less is heard about children with ADD and fewer children are identified as having this condition, which means they have similar difficulties to children with ADHD, but they are not hyperactive. Their attention span will still be very short and they will be inclined to flit from activity to activity without paying much attention to anything. However, they do not do this because they are hyperactive, but simply as a result of an inability to focus their attention. Unlike pupils with ADHD, whose hyperactivity impacts on the learning of those around them, they are a problem to themselves rather than to others.

Sensory Impairment

This term is used for pupils who have a hearing impairment, a sight impairment, or some degree of both. These are known as low incidence needs, because they affect fewer children than the other types of difficulties mentioned so far. There are few children who have no useful hearing or who are registered blind, and even fewer who are both deaf and blind. However, there are many more who have a degree of hearing or sight loss.

Hearing Impairment (HI)

This ranges from a mild or temporary hearing loss, through to profound deafness, where the child may need to reply partly or wholly on signing (e.g. British Sign Language – BSL). Those with some degree of hearing are likely to wear hearing aids. Unlike glasses, these do not always 'cure' the condition, but can help to maximise any hearing the child has. How effective they are will depend on the type of hearing loss they have. For pupils with a more severe loss, cochlear implants are becoming more common, where the child will have an electronic device surgically implanted to amplify their hearing. As with more traditional hearing aids, the effect will vary from individual to individual.

Although there is no reason why a hearing impaired child should not enjoy books as much as any other child, it is helpful to bear in mind that being slower to pick up language will have an impact on their ability to read as well as their peers, particularly when they are younger.

Visual Impairment (VI)

This includes conditions that can be partly, but not fully, overcome by wearing glasses, through to people who are registered blind, in which case Braille may be need to be taught. There are many causes of visual impairment which will determine the type of glasses a child needs and how effective they are in overcoming the problem. In addition, there is a range of low vision aids, such as various types of magnifiers the child may use. Being able to enlarge the size of the font, or using one of the special computer programs for the visually impaired, has made it easier to adapt materials in school for those who need larger print. If children have been taught braille in order to read, books in braille can be borrowed from the Royal National Institute for the Blind (RNIB). Their address is given in Chapter 8.

Multi-sensory impairment (MSI)

This is also referred to as deafblindness. It means that the child will have a degree of both sight and hearing loss. The support they require will depend on the severity of the hearing and of the visual impairment. As mentioned previously, there are very few children who are without any hearing or any sight. MSI is often part of some other condition, such as Profound and Multiple Learning Difficulties (PMLD).

Physical Disability (PD)

This is sometimes referred to as **Physical Impairment** (PI) or **Physical & Neurological Impairment** (PNI). It is easier to spot and to understand than disabilities that we cannot see, but this does not make life any easier for those who have a physical difficulty. It covers a huge range, from those who have a mild form of cerebral palsy, such as ataxia, to those who are wheelchair users. A few with very significant physical disabilities, have to rely on an electronic communication aid, as they are unable to control the muscles involved in speech. Children and young people with PD may require physical adaptations to the environment, in order to access all areas of the school and to enable them to make full use of the facilities.

Newer Needs

So far, we have looked at the main areas of the SEN continuum that have been recognised for some time. To end this chapter, here are some of the more recent descriptions that you may come across.

Foetal Alcohol Spectrum Disorder (FASD)

There has been much discussion in the media and elsewhere about the dangers to a person's health from too much drinking. There has been far less attention paid to the damage a mother's drinking can do to the development of the unborn child she may be carrying. These children may be born with very uneven abilities, so they will perform well in some areas, but be very limited in other ways. Foetal Alcohol Syndrome (FAS) is part of this spectrum and the child will have specific facial features.

Pathological Demand Avoidance Syndrome (PDA)

This is another condition that is gaining recognition. In some ways it is similar to autism. For instance, the child will want to control what happens. In autism, however, this arises from an inability to cope with change leading to an obsession with keeping to the same routines and activities. Children with PDA will appear unco-operative because of an extreme fear of not being in control. They are more socially aware than pupils with autism and know how to manipulate others in order to get their own way.

Premature birth

While it is great that medical science has improved to the extent that babies who are born very early are able to survive, the downside is that there is a growing number of children in school whose learning difficulties are a result of being born very prematurely. Some who are born early do catch up and develop well alongside their peers, but others will have long term SEN. These children may require a very individual approach, as the pattern of difficulties will vary from child to child.

Rare syndromes

Whereas some syndromes, such as **Down's syndrome**, are very well known, an increasing number of children are being identified with a particular syndrome that few others have. How this will affect their ability to learn will depend on which syndrome they have. Contact a Family is an organisation that keeps up to date information in this area (their website appears under 'Organisations' in chapter 8).

Complex Learning Difficulties and Disabilities (CLDD)

CLDD has only been recognised in the last few years. It refers to pupils whose needs are complex because they have co-existing disorders. For example, more and more children are being identified with autism and ADHD; dyslexia and dyscalculia; or SLI, autism and dyspraxia. (NB. This is not a comprehensive list, but just a very few examples of difficulties that sometimes go together). Although the term CLDD covers the whole of the ability range, many of these children will have severe or profound learning difficulties.

And finally...

There will doubtless be other descriptions attached to children's needs, as well as the ones outlined in this chapter, but the greatest change may be in the number of children and young people who are being recognised as having co-existing conditions in various combinations. While there is much still to be discovered, it does mean that schools are educating a more complex population of pupils in terms of their special educational needs and disabilities.

Chapter 2

Current Legislation and SEN Provision in Schools

The changes to the SEN Framework that began in the Autumn of 2010, have been described as the biggest shake up of the system for over 30 years. As a result, the changes are unlikely to be fully implemented until April 2018. The SEN Framework we have at present was put in place as a result of the Warnock Report (1978),[1] which introduced the term *special educational needs*. The 1981 Education Act which followed it brought in the statementing procedures, whereby children and young people with the most complex needs have been given the protection of a statement of their needs and how they should be met. Subsequent legislation has added to the SEN Framework. One of the additions has been the need for every school to have a SENCO (SEN Co-ordinator).[2] This person must be a qualified teacher and, since 2009, has been required to take an additional qualification, which is known as the *National Award for SEN Co-ordination*. Special schools may choose whether or not to have a SENCO, as all their staff are teaching pupils with SEN all the time.

Changing the SEN Framework

Following a preliminary consultation in the Autumn of 2010, in March 2011, there was a consultation on the changes the government wished to make called: *Support and aspiration: a new approach to special educational needs and disability.* A year later, a *Children and Families Bill* was announced, which included the legislative changes underpinning the SEN reforms.

The Bill took the whole of 2013 to go through all its parliamentary stages and became an Act in March 2014. The Act has several parts to it, but by far the largest is Part 3, which was originally confined to children and young people who have SEN. However, a late amendment changed the title of this section to Children and Young People in England with SEN or disability. As mentioned in the previous chapter, while here is a considerable overlap between the two terms 'SEN' and 'disability', they are not synonymous. However, the amendments that were put forward and agreed while the Bill was going through Parliament on its way to becoming the Children and Families Act,[3] means that disabled children and young people are recognised in some of the clauses in Part 3.

Here are some of the main headlines in Part 3 of the Children and Families Act:

➤ Statements are being replaced by **Education, Health and Care Plans** (EHC Plans). They will be extended to cover young people up to the age of 25

---

[1] http://www.educationengland.org.uk/documents/warnock/warnock1978.html

[2] The current role of the SENCO is given in paragraphs 6.84-6.94 of the SEND Code of Practice 2014

[3] http://www.legislation.gov.uk/ukpga/2014/6/contents/enacted/data.htm

> ➤ Local authorities (LAs) are required to produce a Local Offer setting out what provision is available for children and young people with SEN in their area, including educational provision, social care provision and health service provision

> ➤ Parents whose children have an EHC Plan will be offered a personal budget to pay for elements of the additional support their child needs.

The whole thrust of the legislation is to place children and families at the centre, so that they feel more in control of decisions that are made about what is to happen to their child. Although the Act was passed in the early part of 2014, it will take a few years for all the changes to be fully in place.

SEN/SEND Codes of Practice

The previous SEN Code of Practice, which schools relied on to guide their practice, was issued in 2001. It placed the various types of needs children may have under four broad headings:

- Communication and interaction
- Cognition and learning
- Behavioural, emotional and social development (BESD)
- Sensory and physical impairment.

In the current Code, three of these headings remain, but BESD is changed to 'Social, emotional and mental health difficulties', as explained previously.

Another main change for schools is the removal of school action and school action plus. Under the 2001 Code, children placed on school action had their needs recognised and the school was responsible for arranging how to meet them. At school action plus, the school called on outside specialists to help them to put the right support in place. These specialists might be the school's Educational Psychologist, someone from an SEN Support Service, a specialist teacher from another school, (perhaps one with provision for pupils with a particular type of need), or an outreach teacher from a special school. The current Code has removed the need for placing pupils on school action and school action plus and, instead, having just one school category, which, is called 'SEN Support'.

Special Educational Provision

All the main political parties have recognised the need to have a *flexible continuum of provision* in order to meet the very different needs of the diverse group of pupils with SEN. The definition of what special educational provision refers to is that it is:

> '....educational provision which is additional to, or otherwise different from, the
> educational provision made generally for children of their age...'   —Education Act 1996

For the majority of pupils with SEN, this will mean receiving all or most of their support within their mainstream classroom. Others may have some time with a speech and language therapist, a physiotherapist or an occupational therapist, either in a group or individually. Some pupils will be supported by a specialist teacher or advisory teacher, for example, for the hearing or sight impaired, or from a member of a Behaviour Support Team. An increasing number of mainstream schools have developed specialist units or bases within the school. Some of these are for a specified type of need, such as a speech and language base or a unit for pupils with dyslexia. Others will have a more generalised provision such as a learning support unit (LSU), where pupils can spend varying amounts of time depending on the level of support they need. In addition, the school may have contact with an Outreach Service from a specialist unit or nearby special school.

Children with more complex needs may be in a special school. Just over half the pupils who have a statement of their needs are in mainstream schools and just under half are likely to be in special schools, although there are regional variations. Some special schools are known as generic special schools which cater for a wide range of complex needs. Others will concentrate on educating clearly identified needs such as pupils with Severe Learning Difficulties (SLD) and Profound and Multiple Learning Difficulties (PMLD), Behavioural Emotional and Social Difficulties (BESD),[4] autism, or Moderate Learning Difficulties (MLD) plus additional needs. Some special schools are residential and a few of these are open for 52 weeks a year. Special schools are generally on the small side with, perhaps, between 50 and 200 pupils. They may be primary, secondary or all-age schools. Like mainstream schools, special schools have also developed provision for pupils who form a sub-set within the school and need an even more specialised environment.

[4] Social, Emotional and Mental Health Difficulties in the SEND code of practice (2014)

Chapter 3
Strategies for School Librarians Working with SENCOs

As we know, school libraries come in many shapes and sizes and so do SENCO roles and responsibilities. The role of the special educational needs co-ordinator will vary depending on the size of the school, the age of the pupils, the number of pupils with SEN and how many other roles the SENCO has. Small primary schools, for instance, are unlikely to have a teacher whose only role is to be a SENCO, but the head teacher, the deputy head or a class teacher, may take this on as an additional responsibility. There may or may not be other teachers or teaching assistants employed to work with pupils who have SEN on a full or part-time basis. In secondary schools, the SENCO is likely to have this as his or her main role and lead a department of teachers and teaching assistants. The teacher carrying out this role may have some other name to describe what they do, such as Inclusion Co-ordinator or Inclusion Manager.

As mentioned in the previous chapter, since the law was changed, (*Special Educational Needs Co-ordinators (England) Regulations* 2008),[5] the post of SENCO has had to be held by a qualified teacher. In 2009, it became law that every new SENCO in a mainstream school has to gain the *National Award for SEN Co-ordination* within three years of taking up the post. Funding to enable this to happen was provided by the government until 2013/14, but, although the funding will no longer be there after this, the requirement remains. The Award was given this title because the SENCO has a key role in co-ordinating the provision for children and young people with SEN. How far they spend their time teaching pupils with SEN will vary. While Academies and Free Schools have to follow the same rules about SENCOs, independent schools do not and special schools can choose whether or not to have a SENCO.

In the same way that the role of SENCO will vary from school to school, the same could be said of librarians. Smaller schools are unlikely to have a librarian and even less likely to have a full-time person, ideal though this might be. Larger schools may have a librarian and an assistant librarian and/or someone to help with the administration of the library. So, although the strategies that are suggested in the next paragraphs talk about how school librarians and SENCOS might work together, I realise these terms will not be appropriate in many cases. However, the strategies are very general, in the hopes that they will have some relevance even when the roles are carried out by staff with different job descriptions. Unlike SENCOS, it is not a legal requirement for schools to have librarians, or even libraries! Happily, most schools recognise the value of having a central library which acts as a resource for the whole school, in addition to smaller library areas that are a feature of many primary classrooms in particular.

---

[5] https://www.education.gov.uk/.../Education%20(Special%20Educational

Possible strategies for library staff

1. Who is the SENCO?

While there must be a teacher carrying out this role, they may be called something different. If you are new to the school and do not already know who they are, or it is not clear from the way staff are described, make a point of finding out who has the responsibility for pupils with SEN. There can be considerable advantages for these pupils if close co-operation is established between the SENCO and the person or persons responsible for the library.

2. Work as a team

A good working relationship between library staff and SENCO is essential. Where the school has a large SEN Department, it may be that the SENCO will choose to suggest someone on their team to work with you rather than themselves. The importance of the link cannot be overestimated. SEN children need as much, if not more, access to library resources and the library itself as all the other students.

3. What is your SEN offer?

The SENCO may or may not be someone who has a ready understanding of what the library can offer to pupils with SEN, so do make the time to outline your range of resources, your curriculum knowledge and library services and support that you and your staff can offer. This might not be obvious to the SENCO.

4. Establish common ground

Clearly both of you are extremely busy people but finding the time to talk over common issues, your current offer to the SEN Department and of course listening to potential SEN developments and considering ways in which the library might support these in the future can be useful to your most vulnerable users. Perhaps there are groups of pupils, or individuals, who the SEN team think would benefit from using the library and your expertise as part of a more individualised timetable. Timetabling issues, resources, use of teaching assistants and of course procedures will need discussion. It would also be helpful to discuss the nature of their difficulties and how coming to the library might help them in their learning.

5. Clarify your relative roles

Space may well be at a premium in a busy and active school library, what with Sixth Form use and classes or groups booked to use books and ICT work stations so finding times for more SEN students may not always be easy. Understanding and appreciating the specific needs of this group is essential, their behaviour, their motivation and concentration levels may vary widely on occasions. As you gather project collections, find websites, and perhaps create activities and resources, remember that differentiation is even more important for this group whose reading and writing skills may well be problematic.

6. Consider the school's SEN policies and practices

The majority of pupils with SEN will be in ordinary classes in the school but:

- Does your school have additional provision for these pupils?
- To what extent has the building been adapted for wheelchair users?
- Does your school have a Learning Support Unit (LSU), or a specialist provision such as a hearing impaired unit, an autism base, or something similar for other types of need?
- How do you currently serve the needs of these students, and how can you increase your offer to them?

7. Consider your role in relation to individual pupils

Whether or not the school you work in has some form of specialist provision, there may well be pupils who stand out because they have very significant needs. It's always worth seeking clarification about these users. Discuss with the SENCO the pupils who are of particular concern and the policies and practices you can both implement to support their learning and positive use of the library.

8. Pupils who would like to live in the library!

We all know them don't we? While some pupils have to be encouraged to use the library, there are others who would be happy to spend most of their time there, away from the hurly-burly of the playground, or the flow of people in the corridors. Discuss with the SENCO how to balance a need they may have to be away from the classroom or playground for part of the day, with the need for them to use the time productively and to work towards being able to cope with the social setting of a school. (Chapter 5 has more on pupils who need a safe haven.)

9. Pupils who are resistant to reading

Every school has some of these too! At the other extreme from pupils who see the library as an oasis of calm and order in the maelstrom of school life, are those who have the opposite reaction, perhaps because they associate reading with failure and the last thing they want to do is to spend more time with books. Talking with the SENCO may well lead to the creation of useful strategies to reassure them, provide confidence and produce ways of luring them in and keeping them in. (There is more about reluctant readers in the next chapter.)

10. SEN materials for staff

Do you have a staff development collection? What does it contain about SEN provision and strategies? Most schools will have a collection of books for staff to read and to refer to, including, hopefully, some on SEN. It may be helpful to discuss with the SENCO whether the staff library should be part of the school library or housed somewhere else, such as a staffroom. Wherever it is housed, doubtless you will organise it from the library, but do make use of it yourself, as well as the mine of information that is available on the web, in order to find out more about children and young people with SEN.

Chapter 4
Strategies to Attract the Weak or Reluctant Reader

You as a school librarian are constantly trying to find new ways to create a love of reading and an interest in books — aren't you? In the week beginning 24 November 2014, when *The Guardian* newspaper published a series of love letters to libraries, Terry Pratchett was quoted as saying:

> 'The way to get children reading is to leave the library door open and let them read anything and everything they want.'
>
> —Terry Pratchett[6]

Yet, for many pupils who have special needs, learning to read may be one of the skills they are slow to develop. Even when they are 'off the ground', they may find it hard to become fluent readers, who will read for pleasure rather than because they have been told to. Undoubtedly school libraries can be the salvation for some of these pupils. Yet, if they have a negative experience of reading, the library may be the last place they choose to be. So, how can they be enticed through the door?

First of all, it is important to know something about the nature of their difficulties.

- Do they struggle to keep up with all their work, in which case, they may have general learning difficulties and simply be slower to master the skill of reading?

- Have they been slow to develop spoken language and has this had a knock on effect on their ability to learn to read and to write?

- Do they have dyslexia and find it hard to become literate, despite succeeding well in other areas of the curriculum? Alternatively, it may not be that they find reading difficult, but that they seem to have no interest in books. This reluctance could be part of a general disaffection with school. It could be because they come from a background where reading is not seen as important. Or it could be that they find other activities more enjoyable than reading, particularly if they prefer to be very active.

Who is it in school who knows the pupil better than you do? The SENCO, the class teacher, form tutor, perhaps a head of year, or whoever knows the person best, may be able to shed some light on the reasons for their reluctance to have anything to do with the library. If you already arrange for whole classes or tutor groups to use the library, then any 'reluctant' pupils, will be there as well. Every pupil will get an encouraging welcome but do look out for those who do not seem to respond positively. Armed with the information you have gleaned, go out of your way to point out something that is likely to interest them, whether it is a magazine, a book, or something they can find out about on one of the computers. To overcome their reluctance, they too need to discover that the library really is for them, a place where there is plenty on hand to

---

6 *The Guardian* newspaper (w/b 24.11.14) 'Love letters to libraries'

interest and amuse them, and where no-one is going to pressurise them to read particular books, or, indeed, to read at all in the first instance.

Every librarian knows that the more attractive a library looks and the more books and other resources it contains, the more likely the users are to be able to find something that appeals. So here are a few ideas gathered from the many school libraries I have visited or helped to run:

- Make the area look enticing
- Go for variety
- Think beyond books and computers
- Welcome the local community
- Give pupils ownership of the library.

Make the area look enticing

It goes without saying that a library needs to be a bright, attractive environment where it is easy to see what is on offer and to find what you want. A collection of tatty books with only their spines showing is unlikely to tempt anyone, let alone a reluctant reader. Most libraries for secondary students will have computers the children can use as well as an array of books. At one time, there seemed to be a danger that books would be thrown out altogether by the drive to have more computers in schools. Happily, most libraries have now achieved a balance and recognise the need to see reading as being much wider than books. If pupils are researching a topic for their studies, they will be reading, whether they are exploring the web or studying from an encyclopaedia or other non-fiction texts in book or journal form.

Next, there was the tussle between e-books and the more traditional paper-based variety. Luckily, it need not be a question of either/or, but a question of embracing the new while not neglecting the role that traditional books continue to play. So, having a balance is essential in an effective school library. Evidence shows that some reluctant readers are turned on by technology and will sit happily reading an e-book because of the link with technology. If you are fortunate enough to be able to afford some e-book readers, it may well be a bonus for some of these pupils, who are part of a screen-based generation and enjoy accessing books in this way.

Go for as much variety as you can afford

Obviously you will have budgetary limitations, but do what you can to go for variety in term of formats and text levels. Remember too that many readers, essentially the less secure, may go for book series and sequels. Stock all and everything within your agreed stock selection policy. This will include both e-books and the more traditional variety.

Picture books

We all know that these are not simply for our youngest readers. There is now a wealth of picture books available for all sorts of age groups.[7] These can draw in the reluctant reader, who is relieved to find how few words there are on a page and how much there is to enjoy in the

---

[7] See the SLA's *Riveting Reads: Picture Books from 0 to 90* by Marianne Bradnock.

illustrations. Think of the fun that can be had trying to find Wally in the 'Where's Wally?' series and other similar search and find books, including 'Find the Doctor' (Dr Who).

Novelty books

Younger pupils, in particular, love the growing range of novelty books. There are now so many different types, it is becoming difficult to list them all. Their enjoyment stems from the fact that they are interactive. There are pop-up books, lift-the-flap books, ones where you pull the tabs or spin the spinners. There are feely books, scratch and sniff books and books that include sound effects, as well as many others that are less traditional and more attention-grabbing.

Novels – other worlds

'Every Child has the right to an Adventure' —Bear Grylls

When the *Harry Potter* books first came out, I was amazed to see how quite young children would wade through the tomes because they were so keen to follow the story. It is extraordinary what motivation will do and because this will vary from child to child, having as wide a range as possible is essential. This is easier to achieve if you are fortunate enough to have a Schools Library Service operating in your area or in a neighbouring local authority.[8] Fiction loans and project books containing a range of up to date fiction (or non-fiction), carefully selected by professional library staff will be able to refresh your own stock. You can also encourage pupils to use the local library and some schools include visits to them as part of the curriculum.

Graphic novels are good too aren't they? Set out in the style of comic books, they often have particular appeal to reluctant readers who are put off by too many words on a page.

Non-fiction books

Some pupils and students seem less interested in stories and more interested in non-fiction, don't they? Keen on general knowledge or finding out more about a subject that interests them, building up specific knowledge, following a sports team, (usually football), books about their specific collections or interest, will be what attracts these users. Again, there is a wealth of material from the earliest strands of many reading schemes to series on Sport, including Extreme Sports, books about natural and other disasters, books on jobs that people do and series that explain the types of disabilities people may have. It may help those who are wheelchair users, for instance, to see themselves reflected in books and on related websites, as well as helping other pupils to understand what it is like to have a disability.

Whatever range of books you have in your library and however much your budget, do include some audio books with the related texts, as this is a great way to enhance reading skills.

Think beyond books and computers

Although the major attraction of any library should be the books, to make sure there is a reason to continue to keep coming back, pupils with SEN may respond well to other events going on in

---

8 To find out if one operates in your area see the relevant SLA webpage:
   http://www.sla.org.uk/schools-library-services-uk.php

the library, as well as seeing different books on display. Perhaps you do this already but some librarians run weekly competitions, have prizes for the best reviews, get students to help them publish magazines featuring the library, or make sure the library has a column in other magazines or newsletters the school produces.

Special weeks devoted to particular topics, authors or visitors can add interest. Check out the various schemes to get writers and poets into schools.[9] It is usually worth thinking about combining with other schools to put on some of these special events, which need to be organised, where possible, around other topics or activities the school is covering at the time.

Welcome the local community

Inviting in parents, carers and families so that they can understand why the library is important and what it has to offer is usually a good move too. This will give them confidence in you, your role and expertise and may help them to encourage their children to take an interest. It is policy in many schools to encourage the wider community to use the library as well. Clearly 'silent libraries' are often a turn off for many pupils/students with SEN. Achieving that careful balance between making the library popular and keeping a reasonably quiet, working atmosphere, not one where people are afraid to talk, but one where it is a pleasant place to work and just a pleasant place to be is a skill for everyone who runs a school library.

Give pupils ownership

We all like to feel we have ownership don't we? SEN children and students are just the same. It helps to attract the more reluctant readers if they feel the library belongs to them rather than being somewhere they go to, like another classroom. The library is a special non-classroom space. It is a neutral space. Some may welcome being given responsibilities within the library. Many SEN children like to become volunteer library helpers – whether it is keeping the bookshelves tidy; returning the books to their right places; making notices or decorations to brighten up the area; helping to display the books; keeping records of the books that are borrowed; contributing ideas for the development of the library; writing reviews, poems and articles; or helping to select new titles.[10]

Today, reading takes many forms. What turns a beginner reader into a fluent one is practice and, unfortunately, those who need the most practice are precisely the ones who will practice the least, unless we can take an interest in them, in what they want to know about and support them in overcoming any difficulties. In this context, the saying that nothing succeeds like success might be changed to: nothing succeeds like practice![11]

For many more ideas on attracting weak or reluctant readers *From Audiobooks to E-books: Alternative Formats to Engage Non-readers* by Eileen Armstrong and Sally Duncan is an SLA Guideline that looks at all kinds of alternative formats that provide a new and exciting way to bring story to a generation of digital natives – a tool librarians can use to create readers.

---

[9] For example http://www.nawe.co.uk/writing-in-education/writers-in-schools.html or http://www.ukla.org/publications/view/writers_in_schools/

[10] See the SLA Guideline *Terrific Trainees: Working with Pupil Volunteers in the School Library* by Nikki Heath.

[11] See the SLA Guideline *Creating Reflective Readers* by Prue Goodwin.

Case Study One
Woolgrove School, Special Needs Academy

Woolgrove is a special school in Letchworth Garden City, Hertfordshire for over 100 pupils aged 4–11. Originally a school for pupils who have moderate learning difficulties (MLD), roughly half the pupils are now on the autism spectrum and another large group have speech, language and communication needs (SLCN). In addition, there are pupils who have specific learning difficulties (SpLD), attention deficit hyperactivity disorder (ADHD), or a recognised syndrome, such as Down's syndrome. Like the majority of special schools, the population of pupils has become much more complex in recent years, as those with less complex needs, (such as MLD but with no additional needs) have remained in mainstream education. Numbers on roll have stayed much the same, but the nature of the children has changed and become more challenging for staff. A growing number of pupils have more than one diagnosis.

The school's literacy policy

The aims of the literacy policy include:

- To foster an enthusiasm and love of reading and writing
- To provide a rich and stimulating language environment, where speaking and listening, reading and writing are integrated
- To provide opportunities for pupils to become confident, competent and expressive users of language, with a developing knowledge of how it works
- To develop the fundamental skills of language as a means of communication, thus giving access to the rest of the curriculum and providing a vital key for future learning.

Approaches to reading

Reading is taught both discretely and as an integral part of the curriculum. Pupils are encouraged to become confident, enthusiastic, reflective and independent readers. They experience print in a variety of forms and for a variety of purposes. They are encouraged to read for enjoyment, information and interest and to share personal preferences and opinions about books.

There is a whole school approach to the teaching of phonics, based on *'Letters and Sounds'*. In addition, children are encouraged to recognise whole words on sight. This may be done through the use of flashcards, word walls, reading books, or matching games and labels around the school. They participate in shared reading and guided reading, as well as individual reading. Each class has its own small library, but, in addition, every class makes full use of a well stocked and attractive central library in the school.

The school library

Many years ago, when the library outgrew its small room off the main corridor, it was decided to spill out into the corridor. This is a wide space with plenty of light and a view over the school's internal courtyards, where pond and plant life flourish. Low shelving was purpose built so that the children could easily reach the books and see the books on display on top of the low shelves. As the school increased in size, the corridor was extended and extra shelving was put in.

The library houses three discrete sections:

1. The school's **reading schemes**, where books are organised according to the suggested Book Banding levels. Children are placed within these levels depending on their reading level, rather than their age or the class they are in. Pupils can choose from within these levels, although, where they need more time for consolidation, they are encouraged to stick to the same scheme for a time. Their choices and progress are monitored, as are their responses to what they read. They take their current reading book home on a daily basis and parents are also encouraged to report back on their progress. Regular workshops are held for families who want to know more about how to help their children become better readers. The reading schemes include: Pearson's Bug Club, with both online and hard copies; Collins' Big Cat; and Letterland.

2. There is a sizeable **fiction** library in addition to the reading schemes. Children can choose freely of any books that appeal to them. They are set out according to different genres: picture books, novelty books, poetry books, plays, easy novels etc. The novelty books are particularly popular, from the well-known 'Spot' series, to the range of touchy-feely books now on offer. The novelty book section includes several Storysacks, which really bring the stories to life.

3. There is also a large **non-fiction** section and this is organised using a simplified Dewey system that the school has devised. Two catalogues are available in the library. One has pictures of what each section is about as well as the Dewey numbers without the decimal point. There is a second version for older pupils who can manage to read the headings without the need for pictures. Many pupils prefer to take a non-fiction book home, because they want to follow a particular interest and this is also encouraged.

Children have regular access to this well-resourced library within the school. They are encouraged to select, borrow and return books punctually. This is an opportunity for them to be independent and to make personal choices of books that interest them. Children are encouraged to take these books home to share with parents, carers and siblings. As most of the pupils will find learning to read a difficult skill to acquire, there is considerable emphasis on having books around the school, constantly changing the books on display and encouraging pupils to feel that it is *their* library. Pupils take it in turns to act as library monitors, under the direction of the members of staff in charge. Younger classes come to the library together, so that teachers and support staff are on hand if they need help in finding what they want. Older pupils are allowed to explore the library on their own and are taught to use the catalogues to help them find what they want.

The library has a small selection of e-books in addition to those that are part of the reading schemes and there are computers in the area the children can use. There are also DVDs which have replaced the video section and can be borrowed. There is a separate section of the library which is the professional library for staff.

Staffing

The two teachers who share responsibility for literacy are in charge of the library. They are supported by a teaching assistant who makes sure the books are in good repair and a second teaching assistant who puts new books onto the system, so that there is an up to date record of all the books in the library.

Woolgrove is a special school where the staff are determined to ensure every pupil, however complex their needs, develops a love of books and an interest in reading. This has been achieved by having an extensive and attractive library area, which pupils walk through several times a day and which has become an essential part of the school curriculum.

Staffing

Chapter 5
The Importance of Libraries as a Safe Haven

The more variety of good quality and current books there are, the greater the chances that pupils will find something that interests them. But the library can also be a place which pupils with special needs are drawn to, as somewhere they can sit quietly, with or without a book, perhaps to talk to the library staff, perhaps to escape from the hurly burly of the playground or to have time away from their class group, when it becomes too much for them. Mind you the library isn't simply a space to place stressed or even unruly children/students!

Pupils on the autism spectrum, for instance, can find the whole social experience of being with a lot of other people all day overwhelming. Some schools arrange for them to have short breaks away from class in order to prevent them becoming so overloaded and anxious that they have a meltdown. These can be pupils who arrive at school already in a state of anxiety because the very fact of being in school takes them out of their comfort zone and puts them on edge. Some have likened it to being in a country where we do not understand the language and have to struggle all the time to understand what is going on. For some pupils with autism, the breaks need to be very active as this can help them to cope with being on task for the rest of the time. But for others, having a quiet place to go is what makes the difference between being able to cope in school and becoming too distressed to learn.

These children like routines, so they may want a place in the library where they can retreat to with a favourite book, or work at a computer, or be given a job to do. If it fits in with the school and the way the library is organised, this can be a solution to what happens to a child if they are allowed some time out of class. Assuming that the school is fortunate enough to have a librarian, he or she may be able to keep an eye on these pupils while still getting on with some of their own tasks, if a teaching assistant cannot be spared. Later on, some of these pupils may want to help in the library and with their attention to detail and their love of systems, they can be a real asset. The sense of responsibility this can give them enhances their self-esteem and uses their strengths instead of emphasising their differences.

As well as children who are on the autism spectrum, there may be others in the school who are particularly anxious and seek solitude. They may be pupils who are at the withdrawn end of the BESD label as it has been and now, as explained earlier, has become social, emotional and mental health (SEMH). They may have problems at home or there may be events going on in their lives which makes it hard for them to concentrate on their school work. Knowing there is somewhere within school where they can retreat at times and feel safer than when they are in the thick of things, can make a tremendous difference to their ability to cope with school.

There may be other pupils who are vulnerable: children with sensory or physical needs who feel different and may, unfortunately, attract bullying. Increasingly, there are pupils who were born very prematurely and may remain less advanced than their peers and their immaturity can make them vulnerable.

Libraries are usually no longer places where people are told off for making any noise, but if they have a quiet, working atmosphere, or zone, they can provide a safe and welcoming environment for many pupils with SEN. The librarian's role in creating a safe haven for vulnerable pupils should not be underestimated. Librarians may not be therapists, but they can provide a supportive environment and, indeed, become a key figure in some pupils' lives. In contrast to the classroom, which may be associated with a sense of anxiety or failure, the library can provide a non-threatening place where these pupils have the opportunity to experience a break from other pressures. If they are made to feel welcomed and safe by a member of staff who recognises them and responds to their needs, this can help them to cope with the rest of the school day and, in time, to become more resilient and independent.

Chapter 6
Strategies to Support SEN Students at Secondary Level

Most secondary schools put a lot of time into their links with partner primary schools. This is not always easy and how it is done will depend partly on how many partner schools there are and the priority given to enabling pupils to make a smooth transition from their primary school to the much larger environment of a secondary school.

In a primary school, it will often be the Year 6 teacher or teachers who are the point of contact. From the secondary school's point of view, one of a number of staff may take on this link role. Do make links with your school transition team. Try to take a leading role in designing activities for transition students and this can raise the profile of the library in both your own school and in the primary schools with which you are able to work.[12]

Visits before transfer

Many secondary schools arrange one or more visits for pupils to come as a class group, as individuals (particularly where there are pupils who are likely to have difficulty in making the change), or Year 6 classes from different schools coming together. Usually, a morning or day of activities is organised for them, so that they have an idea of what to expect and an opportunity to meet some of the staff who will be teaching them. A tour of the school is likely to be part of the programme and visiting the school library will ideally be included.

Having an introduction to the library on these occasions can be reassuring for less confident pupils or those who have special needs, for whom the environment of a large secondary school may be overwhelming at first. The calm, working atmosphere, the sense of order and the number of attractive resources on display, can help such pupils to look forward to the change rather than dreading it. Even if it is not possible to include a visit to the school library on these occasions, it will be important to have an effective induction programme once the pupils have transferred to the school for their secondary education.

Induction

Do not forget that pupils with SEN may join the school at other times, as well at the start of the school year. In a way, it is even more important to try to arrange an induction for them as well, as they are likely to be transferring from another secondary school and may be finding it hard to join a class where friendships have already been made.

Spending a little time talking to this group, pointing out your display of the picture books for slightly older pupils, as well as pointing them towards a range of easy novels and attractive non-fiction books without too much text are all examples of established good practice. This first visit

---

12 See the SLA's Guideline – *Crossing the Divide: Induction and Transition in the Secondary School LRC.*

can leave a lasting impression and can help to ensure that the library becomes an important factor in the students' lives once they join the school.

It is often said that readers become good readers because of the amount of practice they get. Reluctant readers are likely to get far less practice, partly because reading is more of an effort for them and they will not read as much or be as keen to practise the skill. Yet, the more they can be encouraged, the more likely they are to become fluent at reading and to want to be lifelong readers of books in whatever format appeals to them.

SEN issues

The older the student, the more they can benefit from spending more time in the school library. Increasingly, they will be asked to carry out research into various topics as part of their school work, as well as for homework, not always by using the library of course! By this stage, the range of ability in any class will be very wide and those who have general learning difficulties are likely to be finding it hard to keep up with the work towards taking exams. These may be the very pupils who use the library the least, yet who can benefit from it the most.

Some schools run Homework Study Clubs or mentoring schemes of one sort or another, often based in the library, which, by providing the right support are particularly beneficial for pupils with special needs, or for those whose home circumstances make it hard to study at home. This may be through lack of space, a dearth of books and other resources, or through being in a family where education isn't seen as particularly important and made a priority. There can be a particular value in Homework Clubs taking place in the school library, where students are surrounded by the information they need to refer to, with expert library staff and hopefully teachers too on hand to help those who would flounder if left to complete their homework on their own.

Case Study Two
Southfields Academy

Background

Southfields Academy is a larger than average secondary school for 1,400 pupils aged 11–19 in London, SW19. It has been described as being one of the most diverse schools in the country, with 20% white British and the majority of the rest being from African, Pakistani, Caribbean or a mixed heritage background. Over half the pupils are eligible for free school meals (FSM). A high number have special needs and around 45 have statements (EHC Plans). There is a hearing impaired unit and a unit for pupils with autism or speech, language and communication needs (SLCN). The school also runs a nearby unit for those who are excluded or at risk of exclusion.

The school was one of the first to become a Teaching School and transferred to Academy status in 2012. It has moved recently into a new building, which, at the time of writing, was just being completed. The school library is located near the main entrance, where it is in a prime position for all pupils to access it. There is a separate entrance which was incorporated into the design, so that members of the community could visit without disturbing the rest of the school. The plan is to have links with Adult Education, as well as other community groups and individuals.

The library

The library is staffed by a full-time librarian and assistant librarian. It is housed in a very spacious area, with large windows on two sides making it bright and airy. In addition, there are windows onto the school corridor, giving the library a very accessible feel. As well as the usual shelves of books, the space has been laid out to accommodate the following:

- a large reception desk with a librarians' office to one side
- a bank of 12 computers, which pupils may use via a booking system
- tables and chairs where individuals or small groups can read, write and study
- a central table for a class or larger group to work together
- display racks where the books are changed on a regular basis
- racks for magazines and newspapers
- easy chairs grouped round coffee tables.

In addition, there is a small classroom off the library, which is staffed by a teacher looking after pupils who have been withdrawn from their classes. The Art Department contributes artwork and this helps the pupils who have been involved in helping to create the displays, to feel a sense of ownership. The displays are changed regularly to maintain the pupils' interest and to give more of them the opportunity to contribute.

Once a fortnight, there is an article about the library in the weekly School Bulletin. This is used to feature particular books, such as the favourite book nominated by a class, a pupil or a member of staff. At other times, there may be activities to do or quizzes to complete. There is also a series of special events, such as a Roald Dahl day or a visit by an author or poet. Once a year, the students join in with other schools in the area to organise a Book Award, which encourages them to share their thoughts on the books they have read and agree a shortlist, before taking part in a vote for the winning book.

Approaches to literacy

The whole school has an emphasis on literacy and the library is seen as central to the drive to help a diverse population of pupils to become literate. There are strong working relationships between the library staff, the literacy co-ordinator, the SEN and the EAL Departments, who plan jointly for work on particular themes, or for groups or individuals. The librarian makes a point of stocking lots of stories from different countries, so that there is something for everyone. Similarly, there is a large number of foreign language dictionaries. The school is skilled at knowing which pupils with English as an additional language have other barriers to their learning, although it is harder to be sure which pupils with EAL also have special needs, if they are not literate in their home language and perhaps their parents have had very little education as well.

There is a stock of easy readers, including picture books, so there is something for everyone. Some of these are kept in a Quick Reads separate section, while others are deliberately intermingled with other books, so that pupils aren't embarrassed by making a beeline for a separate section. There are also graphic novels, such as ones about Dracula, which are a favourite with some of the boys.

The librarian runs an induction course for all new Year 7s, so that they know how to use the library and get the most out of it from the time they start at the school. Lessons for Sixth Formers taken by the librarian include how to undertake research. In addition to e-books, the library budget is going to be used to invest in iPads and e-Readers. The Library Management System (LMS) used is Eclipse, which houses the library catalogue, as well as being somewhere for staff and students to write reviews and for the library staff to add messages.

Use of the library by classes and individuals

To maximise the use of the library and to ensure all pupils are aware of its resources, tutor groups take it in turn to use the library for registration in the morning and afternoon. In this way, every pupil becomes familiar with what the library can provide. In addition, there is a booking system for classes, so that teachers can bring classes or groups in for a lesson when they wish to do so, as well as timetabled lessons for study skills. The careers adviser comes for a week at a time and uses either the library or the canteen which is nearby. The library also accepts students on work experience.

Pupils with SEN

Southfield Academy has its SEN policy available online.[13] The library is sometimes used to take in pupils when they are upset and need time away from their classes and peers. Many SEN pupils enjoy reading quietly in the library and for some it is a retreat from the bustle outside. Some of

---

[13] See the school's SEN policy at
http://www.southfields.wandsworth.sch.uk/images/stories/pdf/sen_policy.pdf

the pupils with autism, for example, feel the library is a safe place to be and have a particular spot where they like to sit and read. The librarian has made a point of stocking a selection of books with a high interest/low reading age for KS3 pupils. She has created a number of activities, including quizzes, which make use of fiction and non-fiction material including atlases and dictionaries. These are differentiated at three levels, so that the same activity can be tackled by pupils of different abilities. Teaching assistants use the library for one-to-one or small group sessions, which are sometimes taken by the library staff. These may be for children with learning or behavioural difficulties.

This is a school where every effort has been made to include all the students and to ensure that there is something for everyone including those who have special needs. This has been achieved through staff from different departments working closely with the library staff and the determination of all those involved to place the library at the heart of the school, both physically and in practice.

Chapter 7
Links Between SEN and Behavioural Issues

In the new SEN Code of Practice, September 2014, one significant change is the alteration of one of the four broad areas of need. As mentioned in chapter 2, the categories in the SEN Code of Practice that has been in use since 2001 are:

- Communication and interaction
- Cognition and learning
- Behaviour, emotional and social development (BESD)
- Physical and sensory needs.

The proposal in the first draft of the Code for consultation (Autumn 2013) was to change BESD into social, mental and emotional health (SMEH). In the revised draft of the Code that was consulted on between 16 April and 9 May 2014, this was changed again to social, emotional and mental health (SEMH). In both cases, the idea was to encourage teachers to look beneath the behaviour for any underlying cause. Some pupils whose behaviour causes concern will be known to have a special educational need, such as ADHD, while others will not come within the SEN dimension, but their behaviour will be problematic for other reasons, within the school setting.

One of the first things it is helpful to know is whether pupils behave badly wherever they are in the school or whether it is more noticeable in the school library. If their behaviour is generally unsatisfactory, then, although it may not make it any easier to deal with, you will know it is not to do with coming to the library. Children with ADHD, for instance, will find it difficult to behave appropriately wherever they are, because their hyperactivity makes it hard for them to stay still and to keep quiet for any length of time. Their inattention means that they will have a very limited concentration span or ability to absorb what is said to them, because they do not listen in the first place. Their impulsivity will mean that they act before they think rather than the other way round. This can be disturbing for those around them, as it can interfere with what they are doing or disturb other pupils when they are trying to listen.

The fact that most libraries have a quiet working area or zone can mean that a pupil with ADHD may stand out if the rest of the class is being attentive. However, it is sometimes possible to get them to settle and to concentrate if they are not expected to stick to a task for too long, if they are allowed to move around for some of the time, or to have something that helps them to pay attention. This may be an object known as a concentrator or fiddle toy. Being allowed to fiddle with something actually helps some pupils to concentrate, because it enables them to be active while staying in their place. Some of them will be reluctant readers, because their lack of attention to detail has made it hard for them to become confident readers. Whether or not this is the case, they may still enjoy books and finding out what they are interested in can be a turning point, so that they look forward to coming to the library in order to look at, or read, books on their favourite topics.

You may come across pupils who have ADD rather than the hyperactive bit. They can also be difficult because, left to their own devices, they are inclined to flit from activity to activity without really taking in very much. Again, if you can find a topic or book that interests them, sitting quietly with a book is a wonderful way of increasing their attention span and will help them to learn to concentrate in class as well.

Pupils with autism can become overwhelmed by having to be in the social setting of a school all day and sometimes meltdowns, (when the child loses control), can be avoided if the pupil is allowed to leave the classroom and have a break. A school library, particularly if it is managed by sympathetic staff with time and knowledge of SEN practices, may be an appropriate place for the pupil to be allowed time away from their class. Although younger pupils would need to be accompanied to ensure that they arrive in the right place and their behaviour is calm enough for them to be there without disturbing other pupils, older ones may reach the point where they recognise when they are about to have an outburst and it may be appropriate for them to leave the classroom by prior arrangement.

Some pupils will be disruptive without being under the SEN umbrella. There are many reasons for this. Some seem to enjoy winding others up and will be adept at finding out everyone's weak spot, including those of the staff!

> *There are lots of root causes why students misbehave or fight against authority but there is also challenging behaviour without logical explanation... Why! because it is fun! It makes the day more interesting, enhances reputation, provides entertainment for everyone and is an opportunity to challenge adults and authority safely... Breaking the rules has tangible rewards. It brings praise from friends, excitement and danger, increases adrenalin, releases serotonin.*
>
> —Dix (2010) [14]

It is not easy to remain calm in the face of a child who is deliberately trying to provoke you, but coming down to their level will not improve the situation. While this may mean ignoring the aggravation, it does not mean ignoring the student, but seeing it as a challenge to try to establish a good relationship with them. Most pupils who are disruptive do not actually like the way they are and want to change. It is worth trying to understand them, to enter into their interests and to find some common ground.

Other pupils may be disaffected and unmotivated rather than actively disruptive. If this is the case, it is another challenge to motivate them. First of all, find out whether they are disaffected with school in general or whether there are any aspects they enjoy. This may provide some clues as to what might motivate them. Entering into their interests and pointing them in the direction of material that might further their interest and increase their knowledge may prove to be a turning point.

These few examples illustrate the importance of trying to understand why pupils are behaving in a certain way and to look for the reason rather than simply seeing them as badly behaved. This isn't always easy to do, but it helps if you compare notes with the other staff dealing with the pupils, particularly the SENCO.

---

[14] Dix, Paul. *The Essential Guide to Taking Care of Behaviour.* (2nd ed. 2010) Longmans Chapter 1 p.7.

Chapter 8
Useful Resources and Websites

When talking about resources to do with books and libraries, it is difficult to know where to draw the line, as so much is available. If you are reading this as a librarian, official or otherwise, you are more likely to feel that you don't have enough funding to purchase everything you would like, rather than being concerned about a lack of resources to buy. The tremendous growth in books for children and young people is a case in point. In addition, there are the changes in the way people can read, whether through e-books, e-readers, or simply through surfing the net. So, it's impossible to list everything that might be of interest, even when restricting it to the area of SEN.

I'll start off with the government documents that have been mentioned in the previous chapters and which refer to the changes to the SEN Framework:

Department for Education (2008) *The Education (Special Educational Needs Co-ordinators) (England) Regulations*

Department for Education (2009) *The National Award for Special Education Needs Co-ordination*

Department for Education (2011) *Support and aspiration: a new approach to SEND*

Department for Education (2012) *Support and aspiration: a new approach to SEND – Progress and Next Steps*

Department for Education and the Department of Health (2014) *Special Educational Needs and Disability Code of Practice: 0 to 25 years*

Houses of Parliament (2014) *Children and Families Act.*

Next come a few organisations that are relevant, starting with those mentioned previously:

Contact A Family   www.cafamily.org.uk
This is the best source of information for syndromes and is kept up to date as new ones are identified.

Royal National Institute for the Blind (RNIB)   www.rnib.org.uk
This provides both books written in Braille for people, including children, who are registered blind, as well as many books that are written in large print and can be borrowed.

The following organisations haven't been specifically mentioned before, but are particularly useful in this context:

National Association for SEN (nasen)   www.nasen.org.uk
This is the main organisation that goes across all types of SEN and disability. During 2014, and with the backing of the DfE, it started the *SEN Gateway*, which houses a number of resources including training materials, so is a good place to go for further information.

School Library Association (SLA)   www.sla.org.uk

The School Library Association is committed to supporting everyone involved with school libraries, promoting high quality reading and learning opportunities for all.

School Library Services

Although individual School Library Services (SLS) are less numerous than they used to be, due to cutbacks in funding, it is sometimes possible to draw on a neighbouring SLS and a complete list is available on the SLA website (see above), together with a wealth of other information.

As it might seem rather arbitrary to pick out some books while ignoring others that are equally good, I've decided to mention some of the publishers who have a number of books and other resources for pupils with SEN and/or reluctant readers:

Badger Books   www.badgerbooks.co.uk

Barrington Stoke   www.barringtonstoke.co.uk

Child's Play   www.childs-play.com

Ransom   www.ransom.co.uk

Rising Stars   www.risingstars-uk.com

Routledge David Fulton Books   www.routledge.com

Usborne   www.usborne.com

If you are looking for authors to visit, you could try a charity such as:
Contact An Author   www.contactanauthor.co.uk

For books that have the characters included to bring the story alive for younger readers, there are firms such as:
Storysacks   www.storysack.com

And for pupils who need to have a fiddle toy/concentrator, you could try the well known:
Focus for Fidgets from TTS Group   www.tts-group.co.uk

Finally, if you want to investigate a way of banding books into reading levels (as in Case Study One on Woolgrove School), do have a look at

- Bodmin S, Franklin G, (editors) (2014) *Which Book & Why: Using Book Bands and book levels for guided reading in Key Stage 1.* Institute of Education Press.
  http://ioepress.co.uk/books/language-and-literacy/which-book-and-why/

or the older

- Baker S, Bickler S, and Bodman S. (2007) *Book Bands for Guided Reading.* 4th edition. Institute of Education Press http://www.ioe.ac.uk/about/5826.html

also

- Bickler S, Baker S, and Hobsbawn A, (2003) *Bridging Bands for Guided Reading.* Institute of Education Press
  http://ioepress.co.uk/books/early-years-and-primary-education/bridging-bands-for-guided-reading/